Sing a NEW Song to the LORD Everyday

Daily Devotions of Praise & Worship to Lift Your Heart & Glorify HIS Name'

Gerard Assey

Sing a NEW Song to
the LORD Everyday*:*
Daily Devotions of Praise & Worship
to Lift Your Heart & Glorify HIS Name

By

Gerard Assey

© Copyright 2024 by Author

Published by:
Gerard Assey
19/18, Palli Arasan Street
Anna Nagar East
Chennai - 600 102

ISBN: 978-81-982127-3-3

All Rights Reserved. No part of this publication may be reproduced, stored in a retrieval system, or transmitted in any form or by any means- electronic or mechanical, including photocopying, recording, or by any information storage and retrieval system, without prior written permission from the author.

(Image courtesy- pvproductions from freepik on www.Freepik.com-Thank You)

Table of Contents

Preface

Worship is the highest calling of every believer. It is the heartbeat of our relationship with God and the essence of our faith. In the quiet of dawn, in the stillness of the night, or in the moments between, worship lifts us beyond the mundane and into the presence of our Creator. It is a privilege and a joy, a duty and a delight. Yet, worship is not static—it is ever-evolving, as God continually reveals new dimensions of His love, power, and glory.

This book, **'Sing a NEW Song to the LORD Everyday*: Daily Devotions of Praise & Worship to Lift Your Heart & Glorify HIS Name'***, is born from a deep conviction that worship should never grow stale. It is a call to embrace the freshness of God's mercies, which are new every morning (Lamentations 3:22-23), by offering Him a new song each day. Singing a new song is not just about melodies or lyrics; it is about a heart that recognizes and responds to the unchanging faithfulness of an ever-revealing God.

Throughout Scripture, we find numerous exhortations to "sing a new song." From the psalms of David to the visions of John in Revelation, the command resonates as an invitation to participate in the eternal chorus of heaven. A new song celebrates God's past deeds, proclaims His current works, and anticipates His future triumphs. It is the expression of a heart captivated by God's greatness, humbled by His grace, and overwhelmed by His love.

This book is designed to guide you into a deeper experience of daily worship. Each devotional reflection is crafted to help you meditate on the glory of God, the power of His Word, and the joy of His presence. The themes explore the many dimensions of worship—from its impact on God, to its transformative work in our lives, to its role in inspiring others and uniting believers across the globe.

You will find these reflections rooted in Scripture, drawing from real-life examples, and enriched by timeless truths of faith. They are not just for singers or musicians but for anyone who longs to exalt the Lord in spirit and in truth. Whether you are lifting your voice in song, whispering words of adoration, or meditating silently on His goodness, these devotions aim to ignite a new passion for worship in your heart.

As you journey through these pages, may you discover the profound joy of offering a new song to the Lord every day. May your worship be a sweet aroma to Him, an inspiration to others, and a source of renewal and strength for your soul.

To Him who is worthy of all honor, glory, and praise—may this book glorify His name and deepen your daily walk with Him.

With a heart full of gratitude,

Why Sing a New Song?

Key Verse:
"Oh sing to the Lord a new song; sing to the Lord, all the earth!" – Psalm 96:1

Reflection:
Worship is the heart's response to God's goodness, majesty, and unfailing love. Throughout Scripture, we are called to sing *a new song* to the Lord. But what does this mean, and why is it so important in our lives as believers?

A new song is not merely about composing fresh lyrics or melodies. It represents a renewed response to God's never-ending work in our lives and the world around us. It reflects an awareness of His ongoing acts of grace, provision, and mercy. Just as God's mercies are new every morning (Lamentations 3:22-23), our praise should be a fresh acknowledgment of His faithfulness.

Psalm 96:1 commands, *"Sing to the Lord a new song; sing to the Lord, all the earth!"* This verse calls all of creation to participate in declaring God's glory with fresh passion and gratitude. Singing a new song is not limited to worship leaders or musicians—it is for every believer. Whether in the quietness of your room or among a congregation, your worship is an offering that delights the heart of God.

God's Nature Demands Fresh Worship
God is infinite, creative, and ever-active. The psalmist reminds us in Psalm 40:3 that God puts a new song in our mouths, a song of praise that comes from witnessing His transformative work in our lives. Yesterday's song, while meaningful in its time, may

not fully capture today's testimony. God's blessings are continuous; our worship should be as well.

Consider this: the same God who created the universe also cares for you personally. His hand has sustained you, guided you, and provided for you. Has He brought you through trials? Opened doors you thought were shut? Answered prayers in ways beyond what you could imagine? Each of these moments gives birth to a new song of praise.

A New Song Proclaims His Glory

When we sing a new song, we declare God's greatness to the world. Psalm 96:3 says, *"Declare his glory among the nations, his marvelous works among all the peoples!"* Our fresh worship is not just an act of personal devotion—it is a testimony to others of God's power and love.

Think of how the Israelites sang a new song after God parted the Red Sea (Exodus 15:1-21). Their song celebrated His deliverance and declared His might to all who heard it. Similarly, your new song can inspire others to trust in the Lord, drawing them closer to Him.

Worship That Honors God's Work Today

Every new day offers an opportunity to encounter God's goodness in a unique way. By singing a new song, we honor His ongoing activity in our lives. It's not about being musically gifted; it's about letting the overflow of your heart express gratitude and awe.

Challenge for Today:

Take a moment to reflect on what God has done in your life recently. Identify one specific instance of His grace or provision and let it inspire a new song. Whether it's a simple phrase, a melody, or a heartfelt declaration, offer it to Him in worship.

God deserves more than yesterday's gratitude—He deserves worship that reflects His fresh work in our lives. Let today be the beginning of your journey in singing a new song to the Lord each day.

Chapters 1-10:
What Singing a New Song Does to God

Chapter 1: God's Delight in Fresh Worship

Key Verse:
"He put a new song in my mouth, a song of praise to our God; many will see and fear, and put their trust in the Lord." – Psalm 40:3

Reflection:
Imagine a parent receiving a heartfelt, unexpected word of thanks from their child. The joy that wells up in their heart is but a faint glimpse of how God feels when His children offer fresh worship. Psalm 40:3 reveals that God Himself initiates this act of worship, putting a new song in our mouths. It's an intimate exchange: God blesses us, and we respond with gratitude, awe, and praise.

A new song is more than just music. It's an expression of our personal encounters with the living God. When we sing to Him in the context of what He has done for us, it becomes a deeply personal and unique offering. Every moment of fresh worship carries the fragrance of our individual stories and testimonies, and God delights in these. He cherishes the sincerity of our hearts more than the perfection of our words or melodies.

Consider the power of God's presence in our worship. Psalm 22:3 says that God inhabits the praises of His people. When we sing to Him with a renewed spirit, it creates a space where He draws near. In that sacred exchange, we sense His delight—a joy that surpasses all human understanding.

Think of how King David danced before the Lord with all his might when the Ark of the Covenant was brought back to Jerusalem (2 Samuel 6:14-15). David's exuberant praise wasn't scripted or rehearsed; it was a spontaneous overflow of his love for God. In the same way, when we approach God with fresh worship, it reflects the overflow of our gratitude and acknowledgment of His majesty.

God's Joy in Fresh Worship

Just as a gardener enjoys the beauty of a newly blossomed flower, God finds joy in every new song we sing. He isn't looking for repetitive rituals or hollow routines but for hearts that come alive in His presence. Our worship becomes a fragrant offering, pleasing to Him, as described in Revelation 5:8, where the prayers and praises of the saints rise like incense before His throne.

What makes this new song unique is its relevance to what God is doing in our lives right now. Are you celebrating a victory, experiencing His provision, or marveling at His creation? Sing about it! Let your worship align with God's present work in your life.

Challenge for Today:

Reflect on a specific way God has revealed His love, mercy, or power to you recently. Take those thoughts and translate them into words of praise. Whether it's a simple refrain or a full melody, offer it as a heartfelt gift to the One who delights in your worship.

God doesn't just listen to our songs—He rejoices in them. Every new song is a testament to His goodness and a reflection of our love. Make today's worship a moment that brings joy to His heart.

Chapter 2: Honoring God's Continuous Works

Key Verse:
"Oh sing to the Lord a new song, for he has done marvelous things!" – Psalm 98:1

Reflection:
The works of God are unparalleled, infinite, and worthy of constant praise. Psalm 98:1 urges us to sing a new song because He has done marvelous things. Our worship should echo the unfolding of His miraculous deeds in our lives, our communities, and the world around us.

Think of Israel's deliverance at the Red Sea. After witnessing God's unmatched power in parting the waters, Moses and the Israelites broke into a song of praise (Exodus 15:1-18). Their song wasn't a ritualistic hymn; it was a spontaneous response to God's intervention in their most desperate moment. The lyrics proclaimed His strength, His victory over their enemies, and His faithfulness.

In the same way, every act of God in our lives warrants fresh worship. When we recognize His hand in our circumstances, we honor Him by responding with a new song. It could be as simple as thanking Him for daily provisions or as profound as praising Him for a life-changing breakthrough. Each act of gratitude acknowledges His ongoing involvement in our lives.

Fresh Worship Honors God's Faithfulness

God's works are not limited to history or ancient miracles—they are continuous and evident today. Have you seen His provision in times of lack, His peace in the midst of chaos, or His guidance in uncertain decisions? These moments are opportunities to sing a new song that glorifies His faithfulness.

Fresh worship reminds us of the dynamic nature of our relationship with God. When we honor Him with a new song, we declare that His works are not relics of the past but living realities shaping our present and future.

Challenge for Today:

Take time to reflect on a specific moment when God intervened in your life. Write down how His actions brought you joy, relief, or hope. Turn those reflections into a new song, expressing your gratitude for His marvelous works.

Worshiping God for His continuous works is a way of keeping our faith vibrant and our connection to Him alive. Let your new song today honor the One who never ceases to do marvelous things.

Chapter 3: Reflecting God's Creative Nature

Key Verse:
"Sing to Him a new song; play skillfully, and shout for joy." – Psalm 33:3

Reflection:
From the grandeur of the universe to the intricacy of a single snowflake, God's creative nature is evident in everything around us. As beings made in His image (Genesis 1:27), we are called to reflect His creativity, especially in our worship. Psalm 33:3 invites us to sing to Him a new song and to play skillfully, shouting for joy. This call to creative worship highlights the beauty of expressing our love for God in fresh, inspired ways.

When we sing a new song, we reflect the God who formed the heavens by His word and the stars by His breath (Psalm 33:6). Worship is our opportunity to mirror His creativity through our voices, instruments, and heartfelt expressions.

Creative Worship Reflects God's Glory

Every time we craft a new song, we declare that God's creativity is alive in us. Just as He continually renews His works in creation, we offer Him renewed worship. Think of the psalmists who wrote countless songs inspired by their experiences with God. Their lyrics were filled with raw emotions, personal encounters, and deep revelations.

Creative worship also inspires others. When we sing a new song with authenticity and joy, it can encourage those around us to see God's beauty in fresh ways. Worship becomes a ripple effect, spreading the glory of God to everyone who hears it.

Challenge for Today:
Take a walk outside or spend a few minutes observing God's creation. Let the wonder of His artistry inspire you to create something unique for Him—a new song, a melody, or even a written reflection.

God's creative nature invites us to worship Him with originality and enthusiasm. Let your new song today be a reflection of His endless creativity and glory.

Chapter 4: Proclaiming His Sovereignty

Key Verse:
"And they sang a new song, saying, 'Worthy are You to take the scroll and to open its seals, for You were slain, and by Your blood, You ransomed people for God from every tribe and language and people and nation.'" – Revelation 5:9

Reflection:
Worship reaches its highest form when it proclaims the sovereignty of God. Revelation 5:9 gives us a glimpse into heavenly worship, where the elders and creatures sing a new song to the Lamb, declaring His worthiness to take the scroll and open its seals. This imagery is both profound and humbling—it reminds us that worship is not just an earthly activity but an eternal one.

Proclaiming God's sovereignty through a new song magnifies His unmatched authority and redeeming power. The scene in Revelation is rich with symbolism: the Lamb, who was slain, stands at the center of worship. His sacrifice makes Him worthy to open the scroll, signifying His ultimate authority over history and destiny. Our worship, like the heavenly hosts', should reflect this acknowledgment of His rule.

A new song celebrates the unfolding of God's sovereign plan. Each day brings fresh revelations of how His sovereignty manifests in our lives. Consider moments when He brought order to your chaos, guided you through uncertainty, or redeemed what seemed lost. Singing a new song in response to these experiences is a declaration that He reigns supreme over all creation.

Heavenly Worship as Our Model

The new song in Revelation 5:9 is not just about the past but about the ongoing work of Christ. It acknowledges that He has ransomed people from every nation, tribe, and tongue—a testament to His global and timeless reign. When we sing a new song, we join this heavenly chorus, aligning our worship with what is already happening in the courts of heaven.

By proclaiming God's sovereignty in our songs, we also become witnesses to those around us. Just as the heavenly hosts declare His worthiness, our worship becomes a testimony of His lordship. It encourages others to see His power and surrender to His rule.

Challenge for Today:

Reflect on an area of your life where God's sovereignty has been evident. Consider how He has demonstrated His authority and provision in that situation. Let these reflections inspire a new song that proclaims His supreme rule over all things.

Proclaiming God's sovereignty through worship is both a privilege and a responsibility. Let your song today echo the eternal truth: He is worthy, and He reigns forever.

Chapter 5: Fulfilling God's Command

Key Verse:
"Oh sing to the Lord a new song; sing to the Lord, all the earth!" – Psalm 96:1

Reflection:
Obedience is a central aspect of worship. When we sing a new song to the Lord, we are fulfilling His command, as stated in Psalm 96:1. This isn't merely a suggestion—it's an invitation from God to participate in the sacred act of glorifying Him.

Singing a new song is an act of submission. It demonstrates our willingness to align our lives with His will and reflect His glory. By responding to this command, we acknowledge that God deserves fresh worship every day—not out of obligation, but out of love and reverence for who He is and what He has done.

Worship as a Pleasing Sacrifice
Throughout Scripture, obedience is often described as better than sacrifice (1 Samuel 15:22). Yet, in worship, the two come together. Singing a new song is both an act of obedience and a fragrant offering that pleases God. It shows that we are attentive to His works and eager to honor Him with fresh expressions of praise.

This command also reminds us of God's inclusive nature. Psalm 96:1 calls the entire earth to sing to the Lord. Our new songs connect us to a global chorus of worshipers who are fulfilling the same command. In doing so, we experience the unity of God's family and the beauty of collective worship.

Challenge for Today:
Consider how you can fulfill God's command to sing a new song today. Reflect on a specific area of your life where you've experienced His grace or provision. Let this inspire a fresh melody or lyric that you can offer to Him in worship.

Obeying God's command to sing a new song is a powerful way to express our devotion. Make today's worship a heartfelt response to His call, reflecting your love and reverence for Him.

Chapter 6: Celebrating His Faithfulness

Key Verse:
"Sing to the Lord a new song, His praise from the end of the earth!" – Isaiah 42:10

Reflection:
Faithfulness is one of God's defining characteristics. From generation to generation, He remains steadfast, unchanging, and true to His promises. Isaiah 42:10 calls us to celebrate this faithfulness with a new song—a song that echoes His unending goodness and reliability.

The Israelites' journey from Egypt to the Promised Land is a profound example of God's faithfulness. Despite their doubts and disobedience, He provided for them, guided them, and fulfilled His promise to bring them into a land flowing with milk and honey. Each step of the way, their songs of praise reflected their experiences of His unwavering commitment.

A Testimony to the Nations

Singing a new song about God's faithfulness is not just for our benefit—it's a declaration to the world. It testifies to His reliability and invites others to trust Him. When we celebrate His faithfulness through worship, we remind ourselves and others that God never fails.

In our own lives, God's faithfulness is evident in countless ways. Perhaps He has provided for you in a time of need, healed you from sickness, or given you peace in the midst of chaos. These moments are opportunities to create new songs that honor His steadfast love.

Challenge for Today:

Take a moment to reflect on how God has been faithful to you recently. Think about specific promises He has fulfilled or ways He has sustained you. Let these reflections inspire a new song that celebrates His unchanging goodness.

God's faithfulness is worth celebrating every day. Let your song today be a joyful reminder of His steadfast love and an offering of praise for His unchanging nature.

Chapter 7: Declaring His Glory to the Nations

Key Verse:
"Declare His glory among the nations, His marvelous works among all the peoples!" – Psalm 96:3

Reflection:
A new song to the Lord isn't just a personal act of devotion—it's a proclamation to the world. Psalm 96:3 calls us to declare God's glory among the nations, turning our worship into a global testimony. Every time we sing a new song, we magnify His name and invite others to witness His greatness.

Consider the example of missionaries throughout history who carried hymns and spiritual songs as part of their evangelism. These songs were not merely tools of communication; they were expressions of worship that transcended language barriers and spoke directly to the hearts of listeners. Whether sung in a quiet village or a bustling city square, these new songs proclaimed God's marvelous works, drawing people into His presence.

When we declare His glory through a new song, we also affirm His sovereignty over all creation. The nations may worship various gods or idols, but our worship points to the one true God who reigns above all. Each new song becomes a beacon, shining light into places where darkness once prevailed.

Worship as Witness

Your personal worship has the power to impact others. When you sing of God's glory, you testify to His greatness in ways that words alone cannot. Think of times when a song of worship has stirred your spirit, bringing clarity, peace, or conviction. Imagine how your new song can do the same for others, revealing the beauty and majesty of God to a watching world.

Challenge for Today:
Reflect on how your worship can declare God's glory to those around you. Consider writing or singing a new song that specifically celebrates His marvelous works in your life. Share it with someone as a testimony of His greatness.

Every new song is an opportunity to declare God's glory among the nations. Let your worship today resound as a testimony to His marvelous works, drawing others closer to Him.

Chapter 8: God is Pleased by Authentic Worship

Key Verse:
"Sing to the Lord a new song, His praise in the assembly of the godly!" – Psalm 149:1

Reflection:
Authentic worship pleases the heart of God. Psalm 149:1 exhorts us to sing a new song in the assembly of the godly, emphasizing the joy and purity of genuine praise. This authenticity is not about perfect pitch or performance but about the sincerity of our hearts.

Contrast Abel and Cain, two brothers who brought offerings to God (Genesis 4:3-5). Abel's offering, given in faith and reverence, was accepted, while Cain's, given without true devotion, was rejected. This story highlights a critical truth: God delights in worship that flows from a heart of love and obedience.

A new song is an act of authentic worship because it reflects a fresh encounter with God. It says, "Lord, I see You working in new ways, and I respond with new praise." This authenticity honors Him, showing that our relationship with Him is alive and growing.

Authenticity in Community Worship

Singing a new song in the assembly of the godly creates an atmosphere where God's pleasure dwells. When believers come together with hearts united in genuine praise, the presence of God manifests in powerful ways. Authentic worship becomes contagious, inspiring others to draw near to Him.

Challenge for Today:

Examine your heart as you worship today. Ensure that your praise is sincere, reflecting gratitude and awe for who God is. Let your new song be an offering that pleases Him, given with authenticity and joy.

God delights in authentic worship. As you sing a new song, let it reflect the sincerity of your heart and bring joy to His.

Chapter 9: Elevating God Above Idols

Key Verse:
"For great is the Lord, and greatly to be praised; He is to be feared above all gods. For all the gods of the peoples are worthless idols, but the Lord made the heavens." – Psalm 96:4-5

Reflection:
In a world filled with distractions and false gods, a new song elevates the one true God above all idols. Psalm 96:4-5 reminds us of God's supremacy: He alone is worthy of praise because He is the Creator of all things. When we sing a new song, we declare this truth, rejecting the allure of worldly idols.
Idols are not just statues or ancient relics—they are anything that takes God's rightful place in our lives. These may be material possessions, ambitions, relationships, or even our own pride. A new song helps to refocus our hearts, reminding us that God is greater than anything the world can offer.
Consider the story of Elijah on Mount Carmel (1 Kings 18:20-39). The prophets of Baal called on their god all day with no response, but Elijah's simple prayer to the Lord brought fire from heaven. This dramatic demonstration of God's power left no doubt about His supremacy. Similarly, our new songs testify to His greatness, silencing the false gods of our age.

A Heart Aligned with God
Singing a new song is an act of alignment. It places God at the center of our lives, dethroning idols that compete for our attention. Each lyric becomes a

declaration of His unmatched greatness, drawing us closer to Him and away from the distractions of the world.

Challenge for Today:
Identify any "idols" that may have taken root in your life. As you worship today, let your new song exalt God above all else, declaring His greatness and reestablishing Him as the center of your devotion.

God is to be feared above all gods. Let your new song today affirm His supremacy, declaring His greatness and silencing the idols of the world.

Chapter 10: Joining the Heavenly Chorus

Key Verse:
"And they sang a new song before the throne and before the four living creatures and before the elders." – Revelation 14:3

Reflection:
Worship on earth is a glimpse of heaven. Revelation 14:3 paints a breathtaking picture of the redeemed singing a new song before the throne of God. This heavenly chorus is filled with voices that proclaim His glory, offering praise that is pure, holy, and eternal.

When we sing a new song, we join this heavenly chorus, connecting our earthly worship with the eternal praise of heaven. It is a reminder that worship is not bound by time or space—it transcends them, uniting believers across generations and locations in glorifying God.

Imagine the harmony of countless voices, from angels to redeemed souls, singing a new song that exalts the Lamb. Each note reflects the majesty of God's presence and the joy of being in His eternal kingdom. Our new songs on earth echo this heavenly reality, preparing us for the day when we will worship Him face to face.

Earthly Worship with Eternal Impact

While our voices may falter and our songs may be imperfect, they still delight the heart of God. Every new song we sing is a foretaste of heaven, a practice for the unending worship we will offer Him in eternity. It's a reminder that our lives are part of a greater story—one that culminates in eternal praise.

Challenge for Today:
As you worship today, envision yourself before the throne of God, singing alongside the heavenly host. Let your new song reflect the awe and reverence of being in His presence.

Joining the heavenly chorus through a new song is a privilege and a glimpse of eternity. Let your worship today echo the eternal praise of heaven, bringing glory to the Lamb who reigns forever.

Chapters 11-20: What Singing a New Song Does for Me

Chapter 11: Renewing My Spirit

Key Verse:
"He put a new song in my mouth, a song of praise to our God. Many will see and fear, and put their trust in the Lord." – Psalm 40:3

Reflection:
There is something profoundly renewing about singing a new song to the Lord. When David declares in Psalm 40:3 that God put a new song in his mouth, he points to a spiritual renewal that wells up from deep within. This renewal doesn't come from mere effort but from encountering the goodness of God in a fresh and transformative way.

Consider moments when your spirit felt weary or burdened. Perhaps life's challenges dulled your joy, and even prayer seemed difficult. It is in these moments that God's invitation to sing a new song becomes a lifeline. A new song can reignite the flickering flame of faith, lifting the heart out of despair and aligning it with His life-giving presence.

Renewal through praise is more than an emotional boost—it's a realignment with the truth of who God is. Singing new words of worship declares His faithfulness, reminding us of His power to lift us from any pit. Personal testimonies often reflect this truth. Many believers have shared how spontaneous songs of praise during difficult times brought clarity, peace, and even breakthroughs they could not have imagined.

When we engage in this kind of worship, we allow God's Spirit to breathe life into our souls. Just as a new song declares fresh trust in God, it also renews our perspective, helping us see challenges through the lens of His sovereignty and love.

Challenge for Today:
Reflect on a time when you felt renewed after worshiping God. Today, let your song of praise be an expression of gratitude for His faithfulness. As you sing, invite Him to refresh and restore your spirit anew.

Singing a new song renews our spirit, lifting us from despair into the light of His presence. Let your voice today echo with fresh praise for His goodness.

Chapter 12: Strengthening My Faith

Key Verse:
"I will sing a new song to You, O God; upon a ten-stringed harp I will play to You." – Psalm 144:9

Reflection:
Faith is often strengthened through remembrance, and singing a new song provides the perfect opportunity to recall God's past faithfulness. In Psalm 144:9, David expresses his intention to sing a new song, an act that not only glorifies God but also reaffirms trust in Him. As we lift our voices in worship, we are reminded of who God is and what He has done, reinforcing our confidence in Him for the future.

Music has a way of anchoring memories. A song can transport us back to a moment of victory, provision, or deliverance. For David, every note and lyric were likely intertwined with testimonies of God's power in his life—from defeating Goliath to escaping Saul's pursuit. Each new song became a faith-builder, connecting his present circumstances with God's unchanging character.

Similarly, our songs of praise declare God's faithfulness and remind us of His promises. Singing builds our faith by shifting our focus from our limitations to His limitless power. This act of worship aligns our hearts with the reality of His sovereignty and strengthens our resolve to trust Him, no matter the circumstances.

Challenge for Today:
Take a moment to write or sing a song that recounts a specific instance of God's faithfulness in your life. Let it remind you of His ability to work in your current situation as well.

Singing a new song strengthens faith by keeping God's faithfulness at the forefront of our minds. Let your worship today be a declaration of trust in His unchanging character.

Chapter 13: Overcoming Anxiety and Fear

Key Verse:
"Sing to the Lord a new song, His praise from the end of the earth." – Isaiah 42:10

Reflection:
Praise has the extraordinary power to lift the weight of anxiety and fear, replacing it with peace and confidence in God. Isaiah 42:10 calls for a new song that echoes from the ends of the earth—a reminder that worship reaches beyond our circumstances and magnifies the One who reigns over all.

Consider Paul and Silas in prison (Acts 16:25). Beaten and shackled, their circumstances seemed dire. Yet, in the stillness of the night, they chose to sing hymns of praise to God. This act of worship not only defied their situation but also unleashed divine power. As they sang, the prison doors swung open, and their chains fell off—a literal and symbolic demonstration of how praise can break the chains of fear and anxiety.

Singing a new song shifts our focus from the overwhelming nature of our challenges to the overwhelming greatness of God. Fear diminishes when we fix our eyes on the One who is greater than anything we face. Anxiety loses its grip when we declare His promises through song, affirming that He is our refuge and strength.

When you feel burdened by fear or worry, remember that praise is a weapon. Singing a new song allows you to confront your anxieties with the truth of God's sovereignty and faithfulness. Each note becomes a step toward freedom, each lyric a reminder of His power to sustain and deliver.

Challenge for Today:
If you are facing anxiety or fear, sing a song that declares God's power and promises. Let your worship become a testimony of trust, breaking through the heaviness and bringing His peace into your heart.

Through praise, we overcome anxiety and fear, anchoring ourselves in the peace and strength of God. Let your new song today declare His greatness and power over every worry.

Chapter 14: Deepening My Relationship with God

Key Verse:
"Oh sing to the Lord a new song, for He has done marvelous things! His right hand and His holy arm have worked salvation for Him." – Psalm 98:1

Reflection:
Worship has a transformative power to deepen our relationship with God. In Psalm 98:1, we are called to sing a new song, not just because it is a command, but as a response to the marvelous works He has done. Every act of worship draws us closer to the heart of God, creating a bridge of intimacy between the Creator and His creation.

Consider the marvels of God's deeds: creation itself, His covenant with His people, the deliverance from Egypt, and most importantly, the gift of salvation through Jesus Christ. Each of these demonstrates God's love and faithfulness. When we sing to Him, recounting His marvelous works, our hearts align with His, and our relationship deepens. Worship becomes a two-way interaction where we express adoration, and He reveals more of Himself to us.

Through worship, we move beyond merely knowing about God to experiencing Him personally. Imagine a friend or loved one—true closeness comes not from knowing facts about them but from shared moments of joy, trust, and communication. Similarly, singing a new song allows us to celebrate those moments of divine encounter, drawing us into a deeper relationship with Him.

Worship also opens our spiritual eyes to see more of God's nature. It's in the moments of lifting our voices that we often gain fresh revelations of His goodness, mercy, and power. Singing new songs expresses gratitude for what He has done while fostering anticipation for what He will do.

Challenge for Today:
Reflect on a specific time when God worked marvelously in your life. Let that memory inspire a song of gratitude and wonder, deepening your connection with Him.

Singing to the Lord a new song is an act of devotion that deepens our relationship with Him. As we recount His marvelous deeds, we are drawn closer to His heart.

Chapter 15: Activating Victory Through Worship

Key Verse:
"You are my shield, and the One who gives victory to kings." – Psalm 144:10

Reflection:
Worship is more than a response to God's greatness; it is a powerful weapon in the spiritual battles we face. In Psalm 144:10, David acknowledges God as the source of his victories. This truth is vividly illustrated in the story of Jehoshaphat (2 Chronicles 20), where worship activated divine intervention.
When Judah faced an overwhelming enemy, King Jehoshaphat sought the Lord. God's response was simple yet profound: "The battle is not yours, but God's." Armed with this promise, Jehoshaphat appointed singers to go ahead of the army, praising God with the words: *"Give thanks to the Lord, for His steadfast love endures forever!"* (2 Chronicles 20:21). As they sang, God set ambushes against their enemies, leading to an extraordinary victory.
This account demonstrates that worship is not passive—it is active engagement in spiritual warfare. Singing a new song declares God's sovereignty and shifts our focus from the challenge to the One who reigns over it. Worship builds faith, silences fear, and invites God's power into our circumstances.
In our lives, we may not face literal armies, but we do encounter battles of anxiety, discouragement, and opposition. Singing to the Lord, especially in the face of adversity, becomes a declaration of trust and an invocation of His authority over every struggle.

Challenge for Today:
Identify a current challenge in your life and respond with worship. Sing a song declaring God's victory and let faith rise as you trust Him to fight on your behalf.

Through worship, we activate victory, not by our strength but by God's power. Let your song today remind you that He is the One who fights and wins every battle.

Chapter 16: Drawing Closer to God

Key Verse:
"Draw near to God, and He will draw near to you." – James 4:8

Reflection:
There is an extraordinary promise in James 4:8: when we draw near to God, He draws near to us. Worship is one of the most powerful ways to approach Him, creating an atmosphere where intimacy with God flourishes. Through song, we can express our deepest adoration and open our hearts to experience His nearness.

Imagine a child running to their parent with arms outstretched. The parent does not remain distant but bends down to embrace the child. Similarly, God responds to our worship with His presence. Singing a new song is an intentional act of drawing closer, an acknowledgment of His worthiness and our dependence on Him.

Throughout Scripture, we see this dynamic. David, known as a man after God's own heart, often expressed his desire to be near God through his psalms. In Psalm 27:4, he writes, *"One thing I ask from the Lord… that I may dwell in the house of the Lord all the days of my life."* David's songs reflected his longing for closeness, and God met him in those moments of worship.

In our personal lives, many of us have experienced the tangible presence of God during worship. It's in these moments that burdens are lifted, hearts are comforted, and faith is renewed. Singing a new song becomes more than just music—it becomes communion with the Creator.

Challenge for Today:
Take time to sing a song that reflects your longing for God's presence. As you do, pay attention to how He draws near, bringing peace and joy to your heart.

Through worship, we draw closer to God and experience the beauty of His nearness. Let your song today reflect your desire to be with Him.

Chapter 17: Transforming My Attitude

Key Verse:
"Rejoice in the Lord always. Again, I will say, rejoice!"
– Philippians 4:4

Reflection:
Worship has the extraordinary ability to transform our attitude. In Philippians 4:4, Paul urges believers to rejoice in the Lord always—a call not dependent on circumstances but on God's unchanging nature. Through worship, we cultivate gratitude and joy, shifting our focus from what is wrong in life to the One who makes all things right.
Consider the context of this verse. Paul wrote these words while imprisoned, yet his heart overflowed with joy and praise. This was not denial of reality but a powerful declaration of trust in God's sovereignty. Worship allowed him to rise above his immediate difficulties and embrace the higher truth of God's goodness.
When we sing to the Lord, rejoicing in who He is, our perspective changes. Gratitude replaces grumbling, and joy displaces despair. This transformation happens because worship draws us into the presence of God, where there is fullness of joy (Psalm 16:11). It reminds us of His faithfulness, His promises, and His ability to work all things for our good.
In daily life, worship can break the cycle of negativity and open our hearts to gratitude. Imagine a challenging day when nothing seems to go right. Taking a moment to sing a song of praise, like *"Great*

Is Thy Faithfulness," can realign our focus. Instead of dwelling on the struggles, we remember the blessings. Gratitude shifts our hearts, and joy follows.

Challenge for Today:

Rejoice in the Lord through worship today, regardless of your circumstances. Let a song of gratitude transform your attitude and bring joy to your heart.

Chapter 18: Acknowledging God's Work in My Life

Key Verse:
"Sing to the Lord, bless His name; tell of His salvation from day to day." – Psalm 96:2

Reflection:
Worship is a powerful act of thanksgiving and testimony. Psalm 96:2 calls us to sing to the Lord and bless His name while declaring His salvation daily. Every time we sing praises to God, we acknowledge His hand at work in our lives and give Him the glory He deserves.

Think of the countless ways God has shown His faithfulness. From small, everyday blessings to life-changing miracles, His works are evident. Worship allows us to pause and recognize these moments, reminding us of His active presence in our lives. Singing songs of praise is a way to testify to others and to ourselves of His goodness.

For example, consider the Israelites singing after crossing the Red Sea (Exodus 15). Their song celebrated God's deliverance, proclaiming His power and faithfulness. Similarly, when we sing, we recount the victories He has given us. These songs become a memorial of His work, encouraging us and others to trust Him for the future.

Challenge for Today:
Reflect on a specific moment when God worked in your life. Sing a song that blesses His name and testifies of His faithfulness.

Chapter 19: Fostering Spiritual Growth

Key Verse:
"Sing to Him a new song; play skillfully on the strings, with loud shouts." – Psalm 33:3

Reflection:
Worship is a catalyst for spiritual growth. Psalm 33:3 encourages us to sing a new song and play skillfully, pointing to the intentionality and focus required in worship. Far from being a passive act, true worship sharpens our awareness of God and deepens our understanding of Him.

When we engage in heartfelt worship, we are drawn into God's presence, where transformation takes place. Singing new songs requires us to meditate on His Word and reflect on His attributes, enriching our spiritual journey. Each melody and lyric can become a tool for learning and a means of aligning our hearts with His will.

Worship also cultivates discipline and dedication. Just as skillful musicians practice diligently, we are called to grow in our ability to worship, whether through song, study, or prayer. This growth shapes our character and strengthens our faith.

Challenge for Today:
Choose a song or scripture-based hymn that challenges you to think deeply about God. Meditate on its words, and let it foster growth in your spiritual walk.

Chapter 20: Breaking Through in Worship

Key Verse:
"About midnight Paul and Silas were praying and singing hymns to God, and the prisoners were listening to them." – Acts 16:25

Reflection:
Worship has the power to bring breakthrough, as seen in the story of Paul and Silas. Imprisoned and shackled, they chose to worship instead of despair. Their hymns of praise not only lifted their spirits but also invited the supernatural power of God into their situation.

As they sang, an earthquake shook the prison, breaking their chains and opening the doors. This was not just a physical deliverance but a spiritual victory that led to the salvation of the jailer and his family. Their worship turned a place of despair into a testimony of God's power and glory.

In our lives, worship can break through barriers of fear, doubt, and despair. When we choose to praise God in difficult circumstances, we declare His sovereignty over our struggles. This act of faith invites His presence and power to work in ways beyond our understanding.

Challenge for Today:
Identify an area in your life where you need a breakthrough. Worship God in the midst of it, trusting Him to move powerfully as you praise.

Through worship, we can experience transformation, growth, and breakthrough, all for the glory of God. Let each song of praise be a declaration of His greatness in your life.

Chapters 21-30: What Singing a New Song Does for Others

Chapter 21: Inspiring Others to Trust in God

Key Verse:
"He put a new song in my mouth, a song of praise to our God. Many will see and fear, and put their trust in the Lord." – Psalm 40:3

Reflection:
When we sing a new song of praise to God, we do more than express our own gratitude—we become a living testimony of His faithfulness and power. Psalm 40:3 reminds us that our worship has the potential to inspire others to trust in God. It's not just the words we sing but the transformation in our lives that draws others to the Lord.

Imagine someone burdened by despair hearing your song of praise. They witness your steadfast trust in God despite challenges and are moved to wonder about the source of your strength. This was David's experience as he reflected on God lifting him from the "miry pit" and setting his feet on a rock. His response of worship became a beacon of hope for those around him.

In daily life, our worship can inspire coworkers, friends, or family members who may be seeking answers to their own struggles. A simple act, like singing a hymn or sharing how a song has ministered to you, can plant seeds of faith in others. Even nonbelievers can be moved by the power of genuine worship, sensing the peace and joy that comes from a relationship with God.

The ripple effect of praise is profound. When one person sings a new song, others are drawn into its melody. They see the evidence of God's work and are stirred to place their trust in Him. Let your song become a light that points others to the Lord.

Challenge for Today:
Think about someone in your life who could be encouraged by your testimony of praise. Share a song or story that reflects God's goodness and let it inspire trust in Him.

Chapter 22: Proclaiming the Gospel

Key Verse:
"Sing to the Lord a new song, His praise from the end of the earth." – Isaiah 42:10

Reflection:
Worship is not only a personal act of devotion but also a powerful proclamation of the gospel. Isaiah 42:10 envisions the entire earth lifting its voice in praise to the Lord. Singing a new song declares His greatness to the nations, revealing His character and inviting others to know Him.

Throughout history, songs of worship have been instrumental in spreading the gospel. Missionaries often brought hymns to new cultures, using music as a universal language to share the message of salvation. These songs transcend barriers of language, race, and geography, uniting hearts in the truth of God's love.

When we sing songs of praise, we affirm the redemptive work of Christ and celebrate the hope we have in Him. Each lyric becomes a testimony of His sacrifice, victory, and promise of eternal life. Worship is not just for the sanctuary; it's a way to carry the gospel into the streets, workplaces, and homes.

As you lift your voice in praise, consider how your song can be a witness. Whether sung aloud or expressed through a joyful spirit, your worship can proclaim God's glory to those around you.

Challenge for Today:
Sing or share a song that reflects the gospel message with someone who may not know the Lord. Let your worship be a vessel for His truth.

Chapter 23: Creating a Culture of Worship

Key Verse:
"Sing to the Lord, all the earth!" – Psalm 96:1

Reflection:
A culture of worship begins with one voice and grows into a chorus. Psalm 96:1 calls all the earth to sing to the Lord, reflecting the desire for worship to permeate every corner of creation. When we sing a new song, we not only glorify God but also encourage those around us to join in His praise.
Creating a culture of worship starts in our homes, workplaces, and churches. It's about fostering an environment where praise is natural, frequent, and heartfelt. This can be as simple as starting a family tradition of singing hymns together or leading worship in small gatherings. Over time, these practices cultivate a spirit of worship that influences others.
Consider how the early church modeled this. Acts 2:46-47 describes believers gathering daily to praise God. Their worship was so genuine and infectious that it drew others to the faith. Similarly, when we prioritize worship in our lives, we set a tone that inspires and invites others to do the same.
A culture of worship is also about authenticity. It's not about performance or routine but about hearts that genuinely seek to glorify God. When people see the joy, peace, and transformation that worship brings, they are drawn to participate.

Challenge for Today:
Take a step toward creating a culture of worship in your community. Start with something simple, like playing a worship song or inviting someone to sing with you, and watch as others join in glorifying God.

Each of these themes underscores the outward impact of our worship, showing how it can inspire, proclaim, and unite others in praise of the one true God. Let your new song be a catalyst for His glory to spread across the earth.

Chapter 24: Encouraging the Weary

Key Verse:
"Praise the Lord! Sing to the Lord a new song, His praise in the assembly of the godly!" – Psalm 149:1

Reflection:
Singing a new song not only glorifies God but also brings comfort to those who are weary. Life's burdens can weigh heavily on individuals, leaving them discouraged and drained. However, praise has a unique ability to uplift the spirit and restore hope. Psalm 149:1 invites the assembly of believers to sing a new song to the Lord—a reminder that corporate worship can be a source of strength for those who are struggling.

Consider how a fresh song of praise can breathe life into weary souls. When we sing, we proclaim God's faithfulness, power, and love, reminding others that He is near and able to sustain them. Worship shifts focus away from the challenges of life and toward the greatness of God. For someone feeling defeated, hearing the joyful praise of another can reignite their faith and give them the courage to keep going.

Paul and Silas provide a powerful example of this in Acts 16:25. Imprisoned and beaten, they chose to sing hymns to God, filling the jail with their praises. Their worship not only encouraged one another but also influenced the other prisoners, and eventually the jailer and his household, who came to know the Lord.

In our own lives, we can be vessels of encouragement through worship. A heartfelt song or an intentional word of praise can remind others that

God is still in control, even in the midst of trials. Your new song can be the lifeline that someone needs to persevere.

Challenge for Today:

Look for someone who seems weary and share a song or a word of praise with them. Let your worship encourage them to see God's goodness and renew their strength.

Chapter 25: Declaring God's Kingdom to All Nations

Key Verse:
"And they sang a new song, saying, 'Worthy are You... for You were slain, and by Your blood You ransomed people for God from every tribe and language and people and nation.'" – Revelation 5:9

Reflection:
Worship transcends borders, languages, and cultures, uniting believers worldwide in a declaration of God's kingdom. Revelation 5:9 paints a beautiful picture of heavenly worship, where people from every tribe and nation sing a new song to the Lamb. This reminds us that our worship on earth mirrors the eternal praise of heaven and is a powerful testimony of God's global mission.

When we sing a new song, we participate in proclaiming God's kingdom to all nations. Worship becomes a witness to His redemptive plan for humanity—a plan that includes everyone, regardless of background or ethnicity. It declares that through Christ's sacrifice, all are invited to be part of His family.

In history, songs of praise have often been tools for spreading the gospel. Missionaries carried hymns into unfamiliar lands, using music to communicate the truth of God's love in ways that words alone could not. Today, our worship can still serve as a beacon, drawing people from every corner of the earth to the throne of God.

Reflect on the inclusivity of God's kingdom as you worship. Every time you lift your voice in praise, you join a global chorus of believers declaring His worthiness. Worship is a reminder that His kingdom is advancing, and one day, all nations will bow before Him.

Challenge for Today:
Sing a song of praise with the global church in mind. Reflect on how your worship is part of a larger story of God's kingdom being declared to every nation, tribe, and tongue.

Chapter 26: Witnessing Through Praise

Key Verse:
"Sing to Him a new song; play skillfully on the strings, with loud shouts." – Psalm 33:3

Reflection:
Worship is one of the most powerful forms of witness. Psalm 33:3 encourages us to sing a new song and play skillfully, not for our glory but to showcase the majesty of God. When done with excellence and joy, our worship becomes a testimony of His greatness, drawing others to Him.

Consider how music and praise have the ability to capture attention and communicate truths that words alone cannot. A well-crafted song of praise can stir hearts, break down barriers, and open ears to the message of the gospel. Even those who may not know God can feel the power and presence of His Spirit through sincere and skillful worship.

In our personal lives, our songs of praise are not confined to church walls. They echo in our homes, workplaces, and communities, witnessing to God's goodness. Like King David, who danced and sang before the Lord with abandon, we can use our worship to demonstrate our unwavering trust and joy in Him. Our loud shouts of praise proclaim that He is worthy of all honor and glory.

Your worship is a living declaration of God's love and faithfulness. It shows the world that He is real, present, and active in your life. As you sing and play skillfully, remember that your praise is not only for

God but also a witness to those around you, inviting them to encounter His glory.

Challenge for Today:
Find an opportunity to witness through your praise. Whether through music, words, or your actions, let your worship testify to the greatness of God and invite others to experience Him.

Each of these reflections reminds us that our worship has the power to influence, inspire, and draw others closer to God. Let your new song resound as a testimony of His glory to a world in need of His love.

Chapter 27: Promoting Unity in Worship

Key Verse:
"Ascribe to the Lord, O families of the peoples, ascribe to the Lord glory and strength!" – Psalm 96:7

Reflection:
Worship has a unique ability to bring people together, transcending differences in culture, background, and tradition. Psalm 96:7 calls families of the peoples to ascribe glory and strength to the Lord, painting a picture of collective worship that unites diverse groups under one purpose: to glorify God.

When we sing a new song, we are reminded that worship is not just personal—it is communal. As we lift our voices together, we affirm our shared identity as children of God, united by His love and grace. This unity reflects the heart of God, who desires harmony among His people.

In the early church, worship was a unifying force among believers from different walks of life. Jews and Gentiles, rich and poor, male and female came together to worship the risen Christ. Their unity in praise testified to the world that they belonged to something greater than themselves—a kingdom where God reigns supreme.

Today, our worship continues to promote unity. When we join in corporate praise, we set aside our differences and focus on the One who deserves all honor and glory. Singing a new song reminds us that we are part of a larger body, the family of God, called to stand together in faith and love.

As we worship, let us strive to cultivate unity. Let our praise be a declaration that, despite our differences, we are one in Christ. In doing so, we reflect the beauty of heaven, where every voice joins in unison to glorify God.

Challenge for Today:
Participate in worship with others, embracing the diversity of the body of Christ. Let your praise contribute to the unity that glorifies God and reflects His kingdom.

Chapter 28: Demonstrating Joyful Faith

Key Verse:
"I will sing a new song to You, O God; upon a ten-stringed harp I will play to You." – Psalm 144:9

Reflection:
Worship is a joyful expression of faith, a celebration of who God is and all He has done. Psalm 144:9 captures this sentiment beautifully, with the psalmist proclaiming a new song to God and playing music as an outpouring of his joy.

When we sing a new song, we demonstrate a faith that is alive, vibrant, and filled with hope. Joyful worship reflects our trust in God's promises and our gratitude for His goodness. It is an outward sign of an inward confidence that God is faithful and worthy of our praise.

Joyful faith is contagious. When others see us worship with genuine joy, they are drawn to the source of that joy. It becomes a witness, showing the world that our faith is not burdensome but a delight. King David often worshiped with exuberance, even dancing before the Lord, and his joy inspired others to join in praise.

Let your worship be a declaration of joyful faith. Celebrate the greatness of God with a new song, showing the world that He is the reason for your hope and happiness. Your praise may be the encouragement someone else needs to embrace the joy of the Lord.

Challenge for Today:
Worship with joy today, letting your faith shine through your praise. Reflect on God's goodness and express your gratitude with a heart full of gladness.

Chapter 29: Setting an Example for Generations

Key Verse:
"Make a joyful noise to the Lord, all the earth; break forth into joyous song and sing praises!" – Psalm 98:4

Reflection:
Worship is a legacy we pass down to future generations. Psalm 98:4 calls all the earth to make a joyful noise to the Lord, reminding us that our praise has the power to inspire those who come after us. When we sing a new song, we set an example for our children and grandchildren, showing them the importance of glorifying God.
Throughout Scripture, we see the impact of generational worship. The Israelites were instructed to teach their children about God's mighty acts so that His praise would continue through the ages. When the next generation witnesses our heartfelt worship, they learn to value and prioritize their relationship with God.
Your worship today can shape the faith of tomorrow. When children see adults singing joyfully to the Lord, they understand that worship is not just a ritual but a response to God's greatness. Your example can inspire them to develop their own connection with Him, carrying the legacy of praise into the future.
Take every opportunity to involve the next generation in worship. Let them see your devotion and hear your new song. In doing so, you plant seeds of faith that will grow and bear fruit for years to come.

Challenge for Today:
Involve the next generation in your worship today. Share your new song with them and encourage them to sing their own, fostering a love for God that will endure.

Chapter 30: Joining the Global Church in Praise

Key Verse:
"Sing to the Lord a new song, His praise from the end of the earth." – Isaiah 42:10

Reflection:
Worship unites believers around the world, transcending geographical and cultural boundaries. Isaiah 42:10 calls for praise to rise from the ends of the earth, emphasizing the global nature of worship. When we sing a new song, we join the universal church in declaring the glory of God.
Imagine the symphony of praise that ascends to heaven each day—a chorus of voices from every nation, tribe, and language, all lifting the name of the Lord. This global worship reflects the fulfillment of God's promise to gather people from every corner of the earth into His kingdom.
Your worship is part of this grand tapestry. Every time you sing a new song, you contribute to the global declaration of God's greatness. It is a reminder that you are not alone in your faith; you are part of a worldwide family united by a common purpose: to glorify the King of kings.
Let your praise extend beyond your local context. As you worship, think of believers in distant lands, some of whom face persecution for their faith. Your song is a powerful act of solidarity, joining theirs in exalting the Lord. Together, we proclaim that His glory knows no bounds.

Challenge for Today:
Sing a new song with the global church in mind. Reflect on the unity of believers worldwide and rejoice in the shared mission of declaring God's praise to the ends of the earth.

This emphasizes the collective impact of worship, inspiring believers to glorify God not only for themselves but also for others around them. Let your praise resound, creating a ripple effect that reaches across generations and nations.

Chapter 31:
The Eternal New Song

Theme: Worship That Never Ends
Key Verse:
"They sang a new song before the throne and before the four living creatures and the elders." – Revelation 14:3

Reflection:
Worship is not confined to this earthly life; it transcends time and space, continuing into eternity. Revelation 14:3 gives us a breathtaking glimpse into the heavenly realm, where an innumerable multitude sings a new song before the throne of God. This is no ordinary song—it is a melody born from the depths of redemption, a declaration of the Lamb's triumph, and a celebration of His eternal reign.
The new song described in Revelation is a reflection of the ultimate purpose of worship: to glorify God forever. While we experience worship on earth as a foretaste, in heaven, it will be the full reality. There, every voice will unite in perfect harmony, exalting the Lamb who was slain and is now glorified. This eternal worship is the culmination of God's plan, where all creation acknowledges His majesty.
What makes this new song so profound is that it is exclusive to those who have been redeemed. It is a song of personal testimony, one that angels cannot sing because they have not experienced salvation. The redeemed stand before the throne, singing from a place of gratitude and awe, fully aware of the price that was paid for their freedom.

Even now, as we sing new songs of praise, we align ourselves with this eternal worship. Each time we lift our voices in adoration, we participate in a heavenly reality that will one day be fully revealed. Worship connects us to eternity, reminding us that our purpose is not limited to this life but is part of a greater, everlasting narrative.

Consider the weight of this eternal new song. It is a song that will never grow old, for the glory of God is inexhaustible. With every passing moment in eternity, there will always be more of His majesty to discover, more reasons to adore Him, and more joy to express. Worship in heaven will be the ultimate fulfillment of our deepest longing to glorify our Creator and Savior.

As we meditate on this truth, let it inspire us to worship with renewed fervor. Our earthly songs of praise are a rehearsal for the eternal chorus that will never cease. Let every note, every lyric, and every act of worship today be infused with the anticipation of that glorious day when we will join the redeemed from every nation, tribe, and tongue to sing the eternal new song before the throne.

Challenge for Today:

Reflect on how your worship today is a part of the eternal new song. Consider how the reality of heavenly worship can shape your praise, making it deeper, more intentional, and more joyful as you anticipate the glory of worshiping God forever.

Conclusion

'Sing a NEW Song to the LORD Everyday*: Daily Devotions of Praise & Worship to Lift Your Heart & Glorify HIS Name'*: The journey through this book has been one of exploration, reflection, and worship—a journey that reveals the infinite depths of God's glory and the unending joy of praising Him with a new song. Each devotional, scripture, and reflection has been an invitation to experience the transformative power of worship. Now, as we reach the conclusion, it is time to reflect on what it truly means to sing a new song to the Lord every day and to carry that commitment into our daily lives.

The Power of Singing a New Song

Singing a new song to the Lord is more than a mere act of melody or rhythm; it is an offering of the heart, a proclamation of His greatness, and an act of spiritual warfare. It aligns our thoughts and emotions with His truth, reminding us of His sovereignty, faithfulness, and love. Throughout Scripture, we see the profound impact of this act of worship:

- ✓ **It glorifies God**: Every new song is an acknowledgment of who God is and what He has done. It declares His mighty deeds, celebrates His character, and lifts His name above all else (Psalm 96:1-3).
- ✓ **It transforms us**: Worship renews our spirit, strengthens our faith, and draws us closer to God. It cultivates gratitude, overcomes fear, and fosters spiritual growth.
- ✓ **It inspires others**: Singing a new song declares God's glory to the nations,

encourages the weary, and sets an example for generations to follow. Worship becomes a testimony that invites others to know the living God.

- ✓ Each time we lift a new song, we participate in the eternal chorus of heaven, joining with angels and believers from every tribe and tongue who declare the greatness of our God (Revelation 5:9).

A Fresh Commitment

As we conclude, let us take this moment to commit ourselves to a lifestyle of fresh worship. Singing a new song daily does not necessarily mean writing new lyrics or melodies; it means bringing a renewed heart to God every day. It means offering Him fresh gratitude, new declarations of His faithfulness, and a spirit that seeks His presence with passion and humility.

Make worship intentional: Carve out time daily to focus on God. Whether through song, spoken words, or silent meditation, let your heart overflow with praise.

Look for God's new mercies: Open your eyes to the ways God is working in your life and around you. Let those moments inspire your worship.

Challenge yourself to grow: Worship is not a static act; it is a dynamic journey. Explore new ways to honor God, deepen your understanding of His Word, and connect with Him in spirit and truth.

A Daily Choice

Choosing to sing a new song to the Lord every day is a decision that requires dedication and intentionality. It is a choice to focus on God's glory rather than our

circumstances, to embrace His goodness rather than dwell on life's challenges, and to lift His name above all else.
As you embark on this commitment, remember that God delights in your worship. He inhabits the praises of His people (Psalm 22:3), and your new song is a gift that brings Him joy.

A Life of Worship
Let this be the start of a lifelong journey of praise. As you sing a new song each day, may your life reflect the glory of God and inspire others to join in the eternal anthem of His praise. Worship is not confined to a moment or a melody; it is the essence of our existence. Let every breath, every word, and every action proclaim the greatness of our God.

To Him who is worthy of all honor, glory, and praise—sing a new song every day and forevermore!

About the Author 'GERARD ASSEY'

Gerard Assey is a Graduate in Economics, a PGD in Management (HRD) and holds a Doctorate in Leadership. Gerard holds several International Qualifications in Sales, Debt Collection, Training & Teaching, and is a 'Fellow' of the prestigious 'Institute of Sales & Marketing Management'-UK, a Certified NLP Practitioner, a 'Certified Trainer', an 'Accredited Management Teacher-Behavioral Sciences', a 'Certified Competency Facilitator', a 'Certified Management Consultant'- (the International credentials of a professional management consultant, awarded in accordance with global standards of the ICMCI); and a Certification from the University of Michigan in 'Successful Negotiation: Essential Strategies and Skills'

He is also a Member of the 'National Association of Sales Professionals' backed with several years experience in varied industries, both in India and Overseas. He also holds an 'Etiquette Consultant' Certification from the USA (by Sue Fox, Author of Best Seller: 'Business Etiquette for Dummies'. She has trained some of the top celebrities' world over). He was also a recipient of a scholarship for extensive training in Japan on 'Corporate Management for India'.

Gerard Assey is 'Founder & Chief Corporate Trainer' of the Group: '**Citius, Altius, Fortius Unlimited'**- an organization that **celebrated 20 years of Glorious Service** in 2021, focusing on 3 Core Competencies:

People. Performance. Profit; in functional areas of Sales & Marketing, HR & Organizational Development, covering Recruitment, Training & Consultancy!

Having managed organizations with large Sales Forces in India & Overseas, his specialization cover extensive areas of Sales Training (All levels - Presentation, Negotiation, Key/ Strategic Accounts Management & Managerial Skills for all sectors), Bid Proposal/ Capture Planning/ Management Trainings, Retail Sales, Customer Service & Customer Retention Programs, Training for Prevention & Collection of Debt, Self & Personal Development Programs (Time Management, Teamwork & Team Building, Business Etiquette & Personal Grooming, Leadership & Managerial Skills, People Management Skills, Train-the-Trainer etc), including preparation of Custom-designed Business Manuals for Internal (HR, Induction, and Sales etc) & External use (Instruction, User Manuals).

Gerard has successfully conducted over 6350 Trainings & Workshops (as of Oct '24) all across India, Middle East, Africa, Europe & S.E. Asia. Besides public programs conducted regularly, both in India & Overseas, he has some of the top names as clients whom he services from Single Owners to large Public & Government undertakings, covering all sectors, for their in-house needs.

His website: www.CollectionSkills.com is the only one in this part of the world to be featured in the 'Collections & Credit Risk Magazine-USA' under 'Who's Who in Training' and ranks TOP, along with other websites listed below on most search engines.

Gerard is author of 160 books already (Nov 2024), all the books being available on all online platforms and outlets as E-books and Paperbacks

A few of our business related books:

1. Bite-sized Bits on Commonsense Management
2. Heart to Heart on Life's Principles'
3. How to become a Successful Manager
4. The Sales Professionals' Master Workbook of S.Y.S.T.E.M.S
5. The Professional Business Email Etiquette Handbook & Guide
6. The Professional Business Video-Conferencing Etiquette Handbook & Guide
7. Professional Presentation Skills
8. Exceptional Customer Service
9. Professional Tele-Marketing Skills
10. Professional Debt Collection Skills
11. The G.R.E.A.T. Sales & Service Workbook
12. Sales Training Advantage for Results (*The Ultimate Sales Training Manual to enable you stand out as a S.T.A.R.*)
13. CEO Daily Planner & Organizer
14. The Sales Professionals' Master Daily Planner
15. The Professional Debt Collector's Master Daily Planner
16. My Daily Planner & Organizer
17. MY EMERGENCY INFORMATION RECORD (Family Emergency & Peace of Mind Planner)
18. The Ultimate Therapist & Counselors Planner and Organizer
19. Building an Ethical Workplace
20. Managing Relationships at Work
21. Managing Business Meetings Effectively
22. Effective Delegation Skills
23. Goal Setting for Success
24. B2B Selling by Email
25. Professional Business Etiquette & Grooming
26. Dining Etiquette & Table Manners
27. Effective Networking Skills
28. Grooming, Etiquette & Manners for Teens, Young Adults & Future Leaders
29. Inter-Personal Skills
30. Get Ready, Get Hired!
31. Selling in a Recession

32. Effective Receivables Management in an Economic Downturn!
33. Real Estate & Property Sales Training
34. Credit Sales & Accounts Receivable Management
35. Selling Skills for Real Estate & Property Advisors
36. Take G.R.E.A.T. C.A.R.E!
37. Spa, Salon & Health Club Selling Skills
38. Selling Travel, Holiday & MICE Services
39. Selling Skills for Spa's, Salons & Health Clubs
40. Retailing in Salons & Spas
41. Selling Holiday, Vacation, Tours & Packages
42. The Power of Sales Referrals
43. Selling Luxury
44. Technical Selling Skills
45. Financial Advisors Sales Training
46. Dealing with Burnout at Work Monopolize Your Markets
47. Selling to Affluent Customers
48. Growing up with Grace
49. Financial Selling Skills
50. *The Effective Manager's Guide: Key Skills to Thrive*
51. From Aspiring to Inspiring: A Guide for New Managers on the Rise
52. The Power of Focus
53. Selling with Integrity: Sell Like Jesus The Perfect Role Model!
54. 31 Habits of Champions: Your 31-Day Journey to Greatness
55. Rejecting Grasshopper Talk: From Grasshopper to Giant-Killer-*Defeating Giants Daily!*
56. Navigate the AI-Powered Future of Bid & Proposals: Up-Skill to Stay Relevant with Alternative Career Paths & Opportunities
57. Hiring Sales Winners
58. Present with Impact
59. Success Unlocked: *Breaking Free from Habits that Hold You Back*
60. Complaints to Cheers, Feedback to Gold: Mastering Complaints Management
61. Thriving Together: *Cultivating Diversity, Equity, and Inclusion*
62. Coaching Skills for Sales Managers

63. Soaring to Success in Business & Leadership: Swifter, Higher, Stronger!
64. From Classroom to Podium: A Student's Guide to Powerful Public Speaking & Presentation Skills
65. Developing Self-Discipline
66. The CEO's 31-Day Power Plan: Unlocking Success through Essential Traits
67. Credibility Matters
68. A Winning Attitude
69. Bid & Proposal Management Using AI
70. Sales Forecasting: A Practical & Proven Guide to Strategic Sales Forecasting
71. Elevate & Energize: *50 Dynamic & Fun Activities for Peak Workplace Morale*
72. 'Sales SOS! Sales on Fire! *30 Days to Conquer Chaos & the Nightmares of Success!'*
73. Mastering Sales Managerial Skills: *Building High-Performing Teams & Driving Exceptional Results*
74. Eagle-Eyed Leadership: Unleashing the Power of 31 Lessons from Eagles
75. The Ultimate Employee Training Guide: *Training Today, Leading Tomorrow*
76. Being More Accountable at Work
77. Creating a Culture of Continuous Improvement
78. Effective Questioning & Listening Skills
79. The Power of Value Selling
80. The Growth Mindset
81. Mastering Professional Help Desk Skills
82. The Power to Lead with Empathy
83. Being Prepared: The Key to Unlocking Success
84. Youthful Spark-Youth Energizers, Activities and Games-Igniting the Fun in Youth
85. Ignite your Motivation for Success
86. Elevate Your Executive Presence: *Your Roadmap to Executive Excellence*
87. Smart Decisions: *Mastering Problem Solving with Strategic Solutions for Business Success*
88. Strategic Planning: *Developing and Implementing Strategic Plans to Achieve Long-Term Business Goals*
89. The Power of Stay Interviews
90. Developing G.R.I.T.
91. Adaptability

92. Diagnosis- *A Key Skill for Leadership*
93. The Burnout-Proof Salesperson: *The Master Guide to Preventing Stress & Burnout*- Strategies for Thriving in Sales
94. Learning from Failure: *Keys to Success*
95. Customer Success Management
96. Overcoming the Killers of Motivation
97. The C-Suite Code: *Mastering Skills for Executive Excellence'*
98. Dealing with Difficult Customers
99. Unlocking Your Potential: Mastering the Top 20 Life Skills for a Brighter Future
100. Nurturing Tomorrow's Leaders: *Essential Soft Skills Every Child Must Learn*
101. Lively & Fun Party Games for Seniors & Elders
102. Role Playing for Sales Champions: From Practice to Performance
103. Fun and Exciting Party Games for Kids
104. Case Studies for Sales
105. Role-Playing for Unbeatable Customer Service
106. Case Studies in Customer Service
107. Case Studies in Winning Negotiations
108. Case Studies in Management & Leadership
109. Case Studies in Human Resources & Talent Management
110. CEO Success Blueprint: The Essential Toolkit for CEOs and C-Level Executives
111. The Salesperson's Self-Coaching Guide: *Master Your Own Self-Coaching Plan for Success*
112. Overcoming Procrastination: *Your Ultimate Guide to Stop Delaying and Start Living Your Best Life*

From the Ministry side, Gerard graduated in the very first batch of Charis Bible College-India & had for over 9 years served as a Part-time Faculty at Charis Bible College-Chennai (Andrew Wommack Ministries-Colorado, USA).
He is also a graduate of the Advanced Mentorship Program (AMP) and the Circle Of Ministerial Engagement (C.O.M.E.) of Prophet Jerome Fernando and a Spiritual Son of the Esteemed Prophet.
An accomplished author of several Secular & Christian Books, Gerard has been on the board of a few

international organizations and boasts of being the SON of the MOST HIGH GOD: An ordinary guy following an extraordinary GOD!

...And some of his most recent Christian Books being:

1. A Bouquet of Praises for My KING
2. Christian Jokes for the Serious Religious' Folks!
3. Jesus Healed You!
4. Praise24Ever! (also in Tamil version)
5. The 5G Network of GOD
6. Building Faith over F.E.A.R- FACE EVERYTHING AND RISE with JESUS
7. Hebrew and Greek Praise and Worship Words
8. Godly Mothers' and Grandmothers' Bible Story time for Kids!
9. Miracles of Jesus in Pictures
10. Raise your Praise all 365 Days
11. Thanking GOD with an Attitude of Gratitude
12. Meditating on the Attributes of GOD
13. Puppet Scripts
14. Alcohol Ruins, JESUS Reforms, Renews & Restores!
15. Habakkuk 2:2 Christian Daily Journal, Planner & Organizer
16. ABC of GOD's Word for Handwriting Practice
17. Daily Bible Verse Handwriting Practice (Building Godly Character & Faith through Cursive Handwriting Practice!)
18. Guiding Light: Fun & Faith-Building Bible Activities for Children
19. Rejecting Grasshopper Talk: From Grasshopper to Giant-Killer-*Defeating Giants Daily!*
20. Teen Titans of Faith: *Building Courage, Determination & Christ-like-Esteem*
21. I AM Empowered: *Unleashing Divine Power with Positive Declarations*
22. Be A Solution Provider-*From Passion to Purpose*: *A Biblical Guide to Being the Answer to the World!*
23. Miracles of JESUS
24. Parables of Jesus for a Meaningful Life!
25. A Grateful Heart: Importance of Sharing Testimonies of GOD's Grace
26. Melodies of Worship to JESUS: 31 Songs of Praise & Worship From My Heart to HIS!

27. I AM SO BLESSED!
28. My Daily Cup of Energizer
29. 31 Leadership Lessons *from* Jesus- *The Supreme Leader*
30. Peace Amidst Storms: A Biblical Guide to Conquering S.T.R.E.S.S.
31. Rise Above: 20 Biblical Eagle Lessons for Life's Triumphs
32. Godly Goal Setting: *The FAITHFUL Blueprint for a Purpose-Driven Life*
33. The Profound Attributes of our Mighty GOD: Understanding the 10S's of the Almighty
34. Worship Now, Worship Forever: *A Journey from Earthly Praise to Eternal Glory*
35. Unceasing Praise & Worship: *365 Days to Worship the King*
36. Awakening Praise & Worship: Hebrew & Greek Words to Raise Your Praise
37. Sing a NEW Song to the LORD Everyday: *Daily Devotions of Praise & Worship to Lift Your Heart & Glorify HIS Name*

Besides regularly contributing to business & trade journals, including international ones such as the 'Creative Training Techniques' and the 'Sales News' of the U.S.A, He is also a member of several prestigious bodies & trade associations, having participated in many Conferences & Workshops in India & Overseas.
Prior to his last assignment of leading & managing a large MNC as head, Gerard had a 3-year stint in the Middle East as a Consultant with a leading British Consultancy Firm.

As the past 'Official Country Representative' for the International Business Award- 'THE STEVIES'-(the business world's own Oscar) for about 4 years- he ensured a few Indian companies that qualify for the same every year!

Gerard can be contacted at:
Email: training@Sales-Training.in,training@CollectionSkills.com
Websites:

www.Sales-Training.in
www.EtiquetteWorks.in
www.CollectionSkills.com
www.RetailSalesTraining.in
www.SalesTrainingIndia.com
www.ManualPreparation.com
www.TrainingWithPuppets.com
www.FirstContactAcademy.com
www.SalesAndMarketingRecruiter.com

Our TRAININGS that can help your team

- ✓ **Sales Effectiveness**: Selling Skills for any Sector: Service/ Logistics/ FMCG Realty/ Insurance & Finance/ Media/ SPA's, Health Clubs & Salons/ Key Account Management, Effective Negotiation Skills/ Bid & Proposal Management Skills/ Retail Sales Training: Any Sector (Auto, Jewelry, Clothing, Luxury etc)
- ✓ **Customer Service Skills**-Complaints Handling & Customer Retention
- ✓ **Debt Prevention & Collection Skills**
- ✓ **Etiquette & Grooming**
- ✓ **Leadership & Managerial Skills**
- ✓ **Self & Personal Development Skills**: Presentation Skills/ Effective Communication Skills/Business Proposal Writing Skills/ Problem Solving & Decision Making Skills/ Empowering Secretaries-The perfect PA! (For Secretaries & PA's)/ Effective Time Management/ Teamwork & Teambuilding/ P.R.I.D.E- **P**ersonal **R**esponsibility **I**n **D**elivering **E**xcellence

www.ingramcontent.com/pod-product-compliance
Lightning Source LLC
LaVergne TN
LVHW010118170826
845678LV00012B/2464